THE LIBRARY OF PHYSICAL SCIENCE™

The Properties of Solids

Marylou Morano Kjelle

The Rosen Publishing Group's
PowerKids Press™
New York

For my children, Krysta and Matthew Kjelle

Published in 2007 by The Rosen Publishing Group, Inc.
29 East 21st Street, New York, NY 10010

First Edition

Editors: Daryl Heller, Joanne Randolph, and Suzanne Slade
Book Design: Elana Davidian
Book Layout: Ginny Chu
Photo Researcher: Marty Levick

Photo Credits: Cover © Gregor Schuster/Photonica/Getty Images; p. 4 © Steve Satushek/Workbook Stock/Getty Images; p. 6 Arnold Fisher/Photo Researchers, Inc.; p. 7 Andrew Lambert Photography/Photo Researchers, Inc.; p. 8 © Jeff Greenberg/Photo Edit; p. 9 (top) © Dr. Richard Busch; p. 9 (bottom) © Thom Lang/Corbis; p. 10 © Dr. Richard Kessel & Dr. Gene Shih/Visuals Unlimited/Getty Images; p. 11 © Gail Mooney/Corbis; p. 12 Gregory K. Scott/Photo Researchers, Inc.; p. 13 Custom Medical Stock Photo; p. 14 © Matthias Kulka/zefa/Corbis; p. 15 © Charles O'Rear/Corbis; p. 16 Jon Lomberg/Photo Researchers, Inc.; p. 17 © Myrleen Ferguson Cate/Photo Edit; p. 19 Charles D. Winters/Photo Researchers, Inc.; p. 20 © Christopher Irion/Workbook Stock/Getty Images; p. 21 © Wally Eberhart/Visuals Unlimited.

Library of Congress Cataloging-in-Publication Data

Kjelle, Marylou Morano.
  The properties of solids / Marylou Morano Kjelle.— 1st ed.
      p. cm. — (The library of physical science)
  Includes index.
  ISBN 1-4042-3421-7 (library binding) — ISBN 1-4042-2168-9 (pbk.) — ISBN 1-4042-2358-4 (six pack)
  1. Solids—Juvenile literature. 2. Matter—Properties—Juvenile literature. I. Title. II. Series.

QC176.3.K54 2007
531—dc22
                                                        2005027852

Manufactured in the United States of America

Contents

Solids and Atoms

Look around you. Everything you see is made of matter. There are three basic states of matter. They are liquid, solid, and gas. Some solids are small, like a grain of sand. Other solids can be large, like a mountain. On Earth there are more solids than there are liquids or gases.

All matter is made of tiny particles, or parts, called atoms. Atoms join with other atoms to form **molecules**. Liquid and gas molecules move

Some solids are hard, like these stones. Others, like cotton balls, are softer.

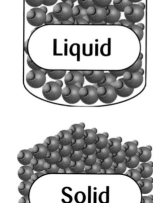

Gas

Liquid

Solid

freely because there is space between the molecules. The molecules of a solid, however, are locked tightly together. This **bond** prevents them from moving far, but they do **vibrate** in place.

The forces of **attraction** between molecules are called intermolecular forces. Intermolecular forces hold the molecules together. Of the three states of matter, solids have the strongest intermolecular forces, or bonds.

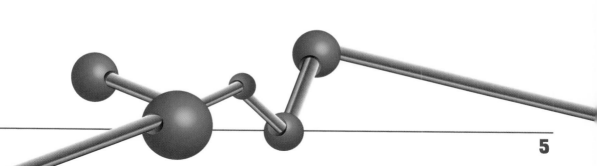

Solids Have No Flow

Solid molecules are tightly locked to each other, and they are also packed close together. There is little space between them. The molecules in a solid have a greater attraction to each other than do those in a liquid or a gas. If you spill a glass of liquid, such as water, it will spread across the table. If you place a solid, such as a pebble, on the table, it will stay in one place. It does not become soft and drip off the table.

A mineral is a naturally occurring solid. Quartz is one of the most common minerals on Earth. Quartz is used to make many humanmade solids, such as glass and special tools.

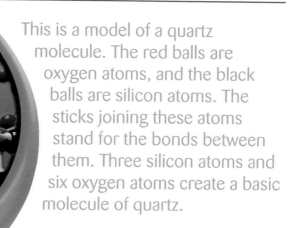

This is a model of a quartz molecule. The red balls are oxygen atoms, and the black balls are silicon atoms. The sticks joining these atoms stand for the bonds between them. Three silicon atoms and six oxygen atoms create a basic molecule of quartz.

Solids do not flow like liquids. The strong bonds, or intermolecular forces, in a solid hold it together and keep it from spreading. A solid keeps its shape. It does not have to be kept in a **container** like a liquid. Can you imagine if your chair were made of a liquid? What would happen?

Physical Properties of Solids

All matter has **physical properties**. Size, shape, hardness, **texture**, and color are all examples of physical properties. We can use them to describe solids. Every pure solid also has a certain boiling point,

Texture is one kind of physical property. Solids have different textures. Some solids, such as the metal bars on your bike, have a smooth texture. Other solids, such as your bike tire, feel bumpy.

melting point, and density. These are all physical properties, too. Many of a solid's physical properties are easy to see and describe. We use these physical properties to help identify the solid. For example, physical properties can help a scientist tell the difference between two metals that look alike, like silver and nickel. By testing the hardness, density, and melting points, a scientist can easily tell which metal is nickel and which is silver.

Solids have strong bonds. Liquids and gases have weaker ones. The strength of the intermolecular forces is another example of a physical property. Physical properties help us tell the difference between different states of matter.

Mineral	Hardness
Talc	1
Gypsum	2
Calcite	3
Fluorite	4
Apatite	5
Orthoclase	6
Quartz	7
Topaz	8
Corundum	9
Diamond	10

Hardness is a physical property, that helps identify solids. Mohs' scale of hardness is a tool scientists use to test the hardness of different rocks and minerals. The softest rock is talc and the hardest is a diamond.

Solids and Shape

Solids come in all sizes and shapes. The shape of most solids cannot be changed. Both the strong intermolecular forces and the fixed pattern of molecules make it hard for solid molecules to rearrange themselves. Only fire or force will change a solid's shape.

Some solids are called crystals. A solid shaped like a crystal has its atoms or molecules arranged in a certain **geometric** pattern. The salt on your french fries and the sugar you put in cookies are two examples of solid crystals. Diamonds are also crystals.

Table salt, which is magnified to 30 times its actual size here, has a crystal structure.

Some solids have atoms that are organized in a **random** way. These solids are called amorphous. "Amorphous" means "shapeless, or lacking a crystal form." Glass and plastic are amorphous solids.

Glass is an amorphous solid that is usually created by cooling a hot liquid substance very quickly. Glass is mostly made of silicon dioxide. This is the same substance that makes up quartz. In quartz the molecules cool more slowly, so they take on a crystal shape.

Solids and Volume

The volume of a **substance** is the amount of space it takes up. Under ordinary conditions most solids keep their shape and take up a set amount of space. Liquids have volume, too, but they have no shape of their own. Gases have no fixed volume and no shape. They will spread out

If you removed all the fish, plants, and rocks from this aquarium, the water level would go down. This is because these things all have volume and take up space in the aquarium.

Here two glasses hold the same amount of water. A golf ball has been dropped into the glass on the right. By measuring the difference in the water level, we can find the volume of the golf ball.

as far as they can and can be pressed into a very small space.

One way that a solid's volume can be measured is by observing how much water is displaced, or moved, when the solid is placed in a large glass tube. The change in the water level tells us the object's volume. Think about the amount of space a whale takes up. Now picture a scuba diver who takes up much less space than the whale. Do you think the scuba diver or the whale will displace more water? What does that tell you about each one's volume?

Solids and Density

All solids have density. Density tells you how tightly packed the molecules are in a solid. The closer the molecules are to each other, the denser a substance is. If two solids of the same volumes have different densities, the one that is

Metals are usually dense solids, with a lot of weight at small volumes. If an anchor were made out of wood or some less dense substance, it would not be able to hold a boat firmly in place.

denser will feel heavier. Solids are usually the densest of the three states of matter.

Did you know that a solid will sink or float in water depending on its density? For example, cork is less dense than water. Cork will float to the water's surface. An anchor, which is often made of a metal such as steel, is denser than water. Therefore, the anchor will sink to the bottom of the  water. A crew at sea will tie a heavy anchor to their ship and then drop the anchor into the water. The anchor will keep the ship from drifting.

Cork is made from the bark of a cork tree. Cork has many air pockets. These air pockets make cork less dense than water.

Freezing and Melting Solids

Sometimes matter changes its state. For example, a liquid can turn into a solid if it becomes cold enough. This is called freezing. The **temperature** at which a substance becomes a solid is called its freezing point. Different liquids become solid at different freezing points. Liquid water becomes solid ice at 32° Fahrenheit (0° C).

When water freezes it takes up more space. Have you ever made your own popsicles with juice? Juice is mostly made of water. If you

On the top is a picture of water molecules in liquid form. On the bottom is water as ice. The molecules in the liquid have no special arrangement. The ones in the ice have an orderly, crystal structure.

fill a popsicle tray to the top, the juice will spill out. This is because the water in the juice takes up more space when it freezes.

A solid will change into a liquid if it is heated to a high enough temperature. Changing from a solid to a liquid is called melting. The temperature at which this occurs is a solid's melting point. When a solid reaches its melting point, its molecules unlock and begin to move freely. The substance becomes a liquid.

Changing from a Solid to a Gas

A solid usually changes into a liquid before turning into a gas. However, some solids change directly into gases. This process is called sublimation. A solid called dry ice can change into a gas. Dry ice is frozen carbon dioxide. Dry ice does not melt. Instead it sublimes into carbon dioxide gas. Have you ever watched a play that had fog or mist on the stage? Dry ice may have been used to create the spooky scene.

During sublimation a solid turns directly into a gas. Molecules of the solid break free from the solid's surface, as shown in this picture.

When a solid sublimates, some molecules escape the strong intermolecular forces and enter the air as gas molecules. At the same time, other gas molecules floating above the solid **collide** with the solid's surface and return to the solid state. This process is called **deposition**.

Unlike ice made from water, ice from carbon dioxide does not go through a liquid stage under normal conditions. This is why it is called dry ice.

Solids and Mixtures

Substances that are made from only one kind of atom are called **elements**. Most matter, including most solids, is a combination of two or more elements. This is called a mixture. In a mixture each substance keeps its original physical properties. This means that mixtures can be separated back into the solids, liquids, or gases that created them. For example, if you made a snack mixture of peanuts and pretzels, you could separate each kind of food again.

A mixture can be made from two solids. Soil, a mixture of rocks and minerals, is a solid-solid mixture. Here three different kinds of soil are shown. *Top:* Silt is a fine mixture of tiny pieces of rock and sediment. *Left:* Sand has larger pieces than silt does. *Right:* Clay often has water mixed in with the pieces of rock.

Some solutions can be made from a liquid and a solid. Pour a spoonful of sugar into a cup of tea, and you've made a solid-liquid solution.

One kind of mixture, called a solution, is created when a solid **dissolves** into a liquid. For example, when you dissolve sugar and cocoa in hot milk you make a solution of hot chocolate. The substances that dissolve in the liquid are called solutes. The solutes in hot chocolate are sugar and cocoa. The liquid in which the solute is dissolved is called the solvent. Milk is the solvent in a hot chocolate solution. Some solids will not dissolve in liquids. These solids are called insoluble.

Solids Really Matter

The chair on which you are sitting, the book you are holding, and even some of the food you ate at your last meal are all solids. There's no doubt about it, solids play an important part in our lives.

Solids will last for a long time and will not change much over time. Solids in the form of million-year-old **fossils** have been found by scientists in many places throughout the world. The fossils allow scientists to see what life was like long ago.

It's hard to imagine a world without solids. Without them there would be no trees or flowers, no houses, no schools, and no hospitals. Without solids there would be no life. It's easy to see that solids really matter!

Glossary

attraction (uh-TRAK-shun) Pulling something together or toward something else.

bond (BOND) What holds two things together.

collide (kuh-LYD) Crash together.

container (kun-TAY-ner) Something that holds things.

deposition (deh-puh-ZIH-shun) The way in which molecules in a gaseous state become a solid.

dissolves (dih-ZOLVZ) Breaks down.

elements (EH-luh-ments) The basic matter of which all things are made.

fossils (FAH-sulz) The hardened remains of a dead animal or plant.

geometric (jee-uh-MEH-trik) Having to do with straight lines, circles, and other simple shapes.

molecules (MAH-lih-kyoolz) Two or more atoms joined together.

physical properties (FIH-zih-kul PRAH-per-teez) The features of a certain substance.

random (RAN-dum) Having no set pattern or order.

substance (SUB-stans) Any matter that takes up space.

temperature (TEM-pur-cher) How hot or cold something is.

texture (TEKS-chur) How something feels when you touch it.

vibrate (VY-brayt) To move back and forth quickly.

Index

Web Sites

Due to the changing nature of Internet links, PowerKids Press has developed an online list of Web sites related to the subject of this book. This site is updated regularly. Please use this link to access the list:

www.powerkidslinks.com/lops/solids/